1	2	3	4	5	6	7	8	9	10
11	12	13	14	15	16	17	18	19	20
21	22	23	24	25	26	27	28	29	30
31	32	33	34	35	36	37	38	39	40
41	42	43	44	45	46	47	48	49	50
51	52	53	54	55	56	57	58	59	60
61	62	63	64	65	66	67	68	69	70
71	72	73	74	75	76	77	78	79	80
81	82	83	84	85	86	87	88	89	90
91	92	93	94	95	96	97	98	99	100
101	102	103	104	105	106	107	108	109	110
111	112	113	114	115	116	117	118	119	120
121	122	123	124	125	126	127	128	129	130
131	132	133	134	135	136	137	138	139	140
141	142	143	144	145	146	147	148	149	150
151	152	153	154	155	156	157	158	159	160
161	162	163	164	165	166	167	168	169	170
171	172	173	174	175	176	177	178	179	180
181	182	183	184	185	186	187	188	189	190
191	192	193	194	195	196	197	198	199	200
201	202	203	204	205	206	207	208	209	210
211	212	213	214	215	216	217	218	219	220
221	222	223	224	225	226	227	228	229	230
231	232	233	234	235	236	237	238	239	240
241	242	243	244	245	246	247	248	249	250

THE CHANNEL ISLANDS

F

FRANCES LINCOLN LIMITED
PUBLISHERS

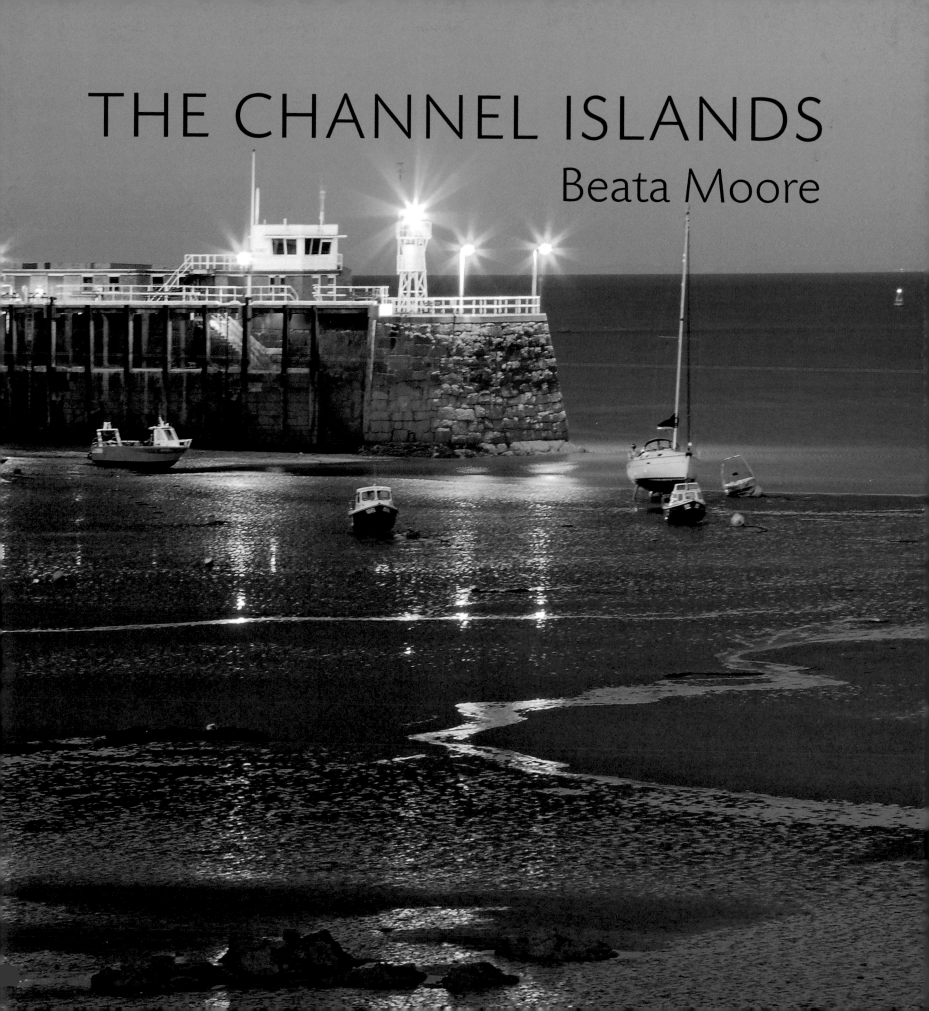

THE CHANNEL ISLANDS

Beata Moore

Frances Lincoln Ltd
4 Torriano Mews
Torriano Avenue
London NW5 2RZ
www.franceslincoln.com

The Channel Islands
Copyright © Frances Lincoln Limited 2011
Text and photographs copyright © Beata Moore 2011
First Frances Lincoln edition 2011

British Library Cataloguing-in-Publication data
A catalogue record for this book is available from the British Library.

ISBN: 978-0-7112-3132-0

Printed and bound in China

9 8 7 6 5 4 3 2 1

PAGE 1 La Rocque Harbour
PAGES 2–3 Gorey Harbour

To my brother Grzegorz, with whom I have
spent many happy days by the seaside

CONTENTS

INTRODUCTION

The Channel Islands are an archipelago in the English Channel. They cover an area of 121 square kilometres (75 square miles) and include the main islands of Jersey, Guernsey, Alderney and Sark, as well as smaller islands like Herm, Jethou, Lihou and many islets and rocks. The islands are situated just off north-west France, approximately 145 kilometres (90 miles) south of England. They are famous for their beautiful coastline and the strong currents and tidal variations. The waters around the main islands are: the Swinge, separating Alderney and Burhou, the Little Swinge between Burhou and Les Nannels, the Great Russel between Sark and Herm, the Little Russel between Guernsey and Herm, La Doroute between Jersey and the continent of Europe and the Race of Alderney between Alderney and the Cotentin Peninsula. These fearsome tidal currents, combined with more than a ten metre- (133 ft-) difference between low and high tide, plus the great many rocks and reefs around the main islands, all make this area incredibly dangerous to all shipping. Despite the close proximity to France, all the islands are subject to British sovereignty but they are not part of the United Kingdom. The islands are divided administratively into the bailiwick of Jersey (comprising Jersey and some smaller islets) and the bailiwick of Guernsey (comprising Guernsey, Alderney, Sark, Herm, Jethou and other small islets).

The islands have a long and complex history. Originally part of continental Europe, they separated from mainland Europe when sea levels rose due to melting ice caps. By around six thousand years ago, the islands were totally cut off from the Continent. Numerous menhirs (large prehistoric standing stones), dolmens (portal tombs) and other archaeological sites indicate that the islands were inhabited in the early Neolithic period. The most famous burial site from this period is La Hougue Bie on Jersey. Some archaeological sites confirm that the islanders were involved in trading with the Continent during the Iron Age, as well as in Roman times. Christianity was brought to Jersey in the sixth century by St Helier, a hermit murdered by pirates in the year AD 555, and to Guernsey by St Sampson. There are many remains of monastic Christian communities inhabiting smaller islands during the same period. The Channel Islands were annexed by the Duchy of Normandy in 933. William I, Duke of Normandy conquered England in 1066 and, as William the Conqueror, became King of England. The Duchy and the islands became part of the English

Crown, however, as the islanders believe, it was England that was added to the islands, not the other way round! In 1204, King John lost the Duchy of Normandy to Philip II of France, but the Channel Islands remained loyal to the British King. As a result they were given many privileges (confirmed by consecutive kings and queens of England) and from that time were governed as separate possessions of the Crown. The last remnants of the medieval Duchy of Normandy can still be traced in the official reference to Queen Elizabeth II, as 'The Queen, our Duke'. Over the years, the islands were invaded many times by France, the last invasion being in 1781. The territorial disputes only ended in the twentieth century when the International Court confirmed that the islets of Ecrehous and Les Minquiers were British. During the Second World War most of the Islands were invaded and occupied by the Germans. During the Occupation, the islands were heavily fortified and on Alderney, concentration camps were built. Many lives were lost there due to slave labour.

The end of the war brought some significant changes to the islands: traditional farming and agriculture and tourism transformed the islands within a very short space of time. A thriving off-shore financial industry furthered the islands' fast development. Whilst English is the official language in the islands, both English and French are widely used. Additionally there are also four old Norman French languages spoken: Jèrriais in Jersey, Dgèrnésiais in Guernsey, Auregnais in Alderney and Sercquiais in Sark. These languages are quite unlike modern French and more similar to the language spoken some nine hundred years ago in Normandy. Despite the close proximity of the islands to each other, there are many differences between them and there is great inter-island rivalry. This rivalry may be seen in the unique nicknames given to each of the islands' residents; 'Donkeys' for the people of Guernsey, 'Toads' for the people of Jersey, 'Crows' for Sark and 'Rabbits' for Alderney.

The fascinating history that shaped the islands, the relics of their Neolithic, medieval, Elizabethan and Georgian past, the fortifications from the Second World War, the fabulous fresh food and colourful customs, the rich heritage of birds and animals, fantastic fishing, sailing and diving sites combined with the laid-back approach of the locals make these islands unique and much-loved by tourists and islanders alike.

La Rocco Tower at St Ouen's Bay, Jersey

Elizabeth Castle, St Helier

Jersey

JERSEY

Jersey is the largest of the Channel Islands. It is 16 kilometres (10 miles) east to west and 9.6 kilometres (6 miles) north to south and lies 22.5 kilometres (14 miles) from the Cotentin Peninsula in Normandy. The island's patron is St Helier, a sixth-century hermit decapitated by pirates who attacked the island. That, however, did not stop St Helier from picking up his head and scaring off the invaders (according to local legend anyway). The Jersey coastline grows and shrinks with the tide by more than 12 metres (39 ft), exposing some amazing golden beaches and mysterious caves. Long beaches washed by Gulf Stream waters, combined with a mild climate and good food make the island a popular place to live and holiday. Jersey has been an island for over eight thousand years and for at least two hundred and fifty thousand years hunters used it as their base. Many ancient burial sites indicate that numerous communities settled here in the Neolithic period. Jersey, like the other Channel Islands became part of England in 1066. The official languages are English and French, but Jèrriais, a form of the ancient Norman language, is also spoken.

Jersey's main town is St Helier, which was most probably established during Roman times. Until the eighteenth century it developed slowly alongside the coast but with growing wealth from privateering, agricultural sales and developing trade, the town spread rapidly inland. The old part of the town is dominated by Regency and Victorian buildings. The Old Market Square, next to the eleventh-century church of St Helier, was renamed the Royal Square in commemoration of George II who influenced the development of the local harbour. He is commemorated in the form of a gilded statue, posing as a roman emperor, erected here in 1751, and from which all distances in Jersey are measured. The Square is overlooked by the imposing States Chamber and the Royal Court House. It was also here that the last battle on British soil, the famous 'Battle of Jersey', was fought in 1781. It was a short but fierce battle. French forces under Baron de Rullecourt landed at La Rocque. The Lord Lieutenant of Jersey surrendered, but courageous Major Francis Pierson attacked the enemy. Both Pierson and De Rullecourt died in battle and the French were defeated. Another important square in the heart of the town is Liberation Square in front of the harbour. The main focus of the square is the sculpture commemorating the 50th Anniversary of Jersey's liberation: a group of islanders with the Union Jack flag is centred in the fountain surrounded by twelve water jets symbolizing the parishes of the island. Overlooking the square is Fort Regent, a fortified garrison designed by John Humfrey in 1806, which has been converted into a leisure centre.

In St Aubin's Bay, in front of St Helier harbour, is the magnificent Elizabeth Castle. Situated on a rocky islet, this fortified structure has over 300 years' history. Built in 1590 by Sir Walter Raleigh, it was named 'Fort Isabella Bellissima' after Queen Elizabeth I. It soon became an official residence of the governors of Jersey as well as a garrison. In 1923 the castle was turned into a museum. Exhibitions in the grounds explain the castle's important military role, while a visit to the rocky ledge where St Helier used to live as a hermit offers a glimpse into the very beginning of the town.

There are many attractions on the island; perhaps the most ancient and mysterious is La Hougue Bie situated in the parish of Grouville. It is possibly the best preserved Neolithic burial site in Europe. It dates from 4,000 years BC and it served a number of ceremonial functions. The name is most probably Norse in origin meaning 'homestead on the mound'. Its long and low passage opens up into a main chamber, while to the north and south there are two additional side chambers that were used as burial plots. The most intriguing thing about the grave is that it was constructed with an alignment to the rising sun on the morning of the equinoxes. In the twelfth century the west of the burial site was topped by a Christian chapel, the Notre Dame; followed by the building of the Jerusalem Chapel on the eastern side in 1520. In the sixteenth century, the new owner of the mound, Philippe d'Auvergne built a gothic tower here and used the chapels as a private place of worship and a library. The tower quickly became a local landmark but with time it became derelict and La Société Jersiaise who took charge of the mound demolished it in 1924. That allowed them to excavate the long passage, the Great Chamber and two side cells. Today the site also houses the island's Archeology and Geology Museum.

A short trip to the east of the island leads to the headland above Gorey village. This area has been occupied since prehistoric times, but in 1204, after losing Normandy, King John sited a major fortified castle here to counteract against a possible future invasion by the French. The sea and cliffs protected the castle from three sides and the granite base was indestructible. The magnificent medieval Mount Orgueil Castle overlooking Gorey village is one of the best known Jersey landmarks. Over the years the castle's role has changed; since its usefulness as a defensive structure ended after new, more powerful cannons were invented, the castle has been used as a barracks, prison and most recently as a museum. It re-opened in 2009 and showcases its colourful past and espionage secrets within its towers and rooms.

Another castle on a much smaller scale is Grosnez Castle. Its ruins occupy the north-westerly point of Jersey, at Les Landes. This picturesque ruin is close to

Le Pinacle, the 70 metre- (200 ft-) high rock that was used as a ceremonial site in ancient times. The castle was built around 1330 but deteriorated significantly over time and today all that remains is a gatehouse. Large numbers of stones from the castle were used for building St Ouen's Manor in 1483.

In the south-west of the island is La Corbière Lighthouse, the first concrete lighthouse in the British Isles. Built on the granite outcrop off Corbière in 1874, it was designed by Sir John Coode. It has successfully withstood ferocious storms in this windy location. La Corbière (meaning 'the place where crows congregate') was the terminus of the train from St Helier between 1885–1935.

The island offers many other attractions, such as a lavender farm where over eighty varieties of lavender are grown across nine hundred acres; the Noirmont Command Bunker from where the coastal artillery Batterie Lothringen was controlled; the Jersey War Tunnels, which detail the story of the German Occupation; the Durrel Wildlife Conservation Trust; the sixth-century St Brelade's Church and Fisherman's Chapel, with its fourteenth-century wall paintings; Quetivel Mill dating from 1309; the Jersey Museum, which recounts the history of life on Jersey; the immaculate gardens of Samarès Manor, Hamptonne Country Life Museum and much more. The most compelling thing about the island, however, is its coastline, rugged in the north, guarded by medieval castles in the east and south and peppered with martello towers in the west. All its 72.5 kilometres (45 miles) of coastline are fascinating, not only because of its natural beauty but also because of these interesting towers. Twenty-four out of thirty-one towers built by General Henry Seymour Conway are still standing around Jersey. The very first was built in 1778 in Grève de Lecq according to the design of the famous round gun tower at Martella in Corsica, but the best-known and arguably the most beautiful, is La Rocco. In the warm light of the sunset this massive granite construction in St Ouen's Bay is undoubtedly an unforgettable view.

Close to Jersey there are many islands, one of them is Green Island or La Motte as it is sometimes called. It is situated on the south-east coast of Jersey and at low tide is accessible on foot. There are also some archeological remains here. Many interesting rocks surround this grassy island.

Les Pierres de Lecq or the Paternosters is a group of rocks between Jersey and Sark. Declared a Ramsar site in 2005, the rocks have the widest tidal range in the world. At a high tide of twelve metres (13 ft) only three rocks are visible, the Eastern One (L'Etaithe), the Big One (La Grôsse) and the Western One (La Vouêtaîthe). At low tide extensive reef and rocks support a variety of cetaceans. The name Paternosters owes its origin to the custom of sailors repeating the Lord's Prayer when passing these rocks. This prayer is said in memory of several Jersey families who, on the way to colonize Sark in the sixteenth century, perished when their boat hit the rocks and sank. The cries of the drowned women and children, so the legend says, can still be heard during storms.

Les Dirouilles islands are also known as Les Pierres. Positioned to the north-east of Jersey, these are a range of lesser known rocks while the Ecrehous archipelago of tiny islets and rocks located 9.6 kilometres (six miles) north-east of Jersey are probably the most visited offshore islands. The three main islands, Marmotier, La Maître Île and La Blanche Île have been occupied on and off since the tenth century. The church and the priory built on La Maître Île by the Abbey of Valricher fell into ruin in the fifteenth century. Since then, the islands have only been used by smugglers and fishermen as well as local eccentrics, like Philippe Pinel who proclaimed himself the King of the Ecrehous. He lived on Bliantch Île between 1848–98. This tiny island covers an area of approximately four square metres (13 square feet) at low tide and significantly less at high tide. The charm of these islets lie in the crystal clear water, the lunar-style landscape appearing at the low tide and the privately-owned fishermen's grey-stone and white-washed huts. The largest house on the island is the Custom House which belongs to the State of Jersey. The sovereignty of the islands was disputed for centuries and eventually Great Britain and France went to the International Court of Justice in 1950. Based on historical evidence, the Court awarded the islands to Jersey. Despite this, now and again there are French 'invasions'. In 1993 and in 1994, 'invaders' raised the Norman flag and tried to claim the islets as a part of France. The idea, however, was quickly forgotten after a priest celebrated mass and the invaders left the island peacefully.

The Minquiers are situated 14.5 kilometres (9 miles) south of Jersey and are the southernmost territory in the British Isles. These small islets, with no permanent inhabitants, contain only a few buildings used by fishermen for shelter. Two larger islands are visited during the summer time by yachtsmen and vraic (seaweed) collectors. Like Ecrehous, in 1953 the Minquiers were awarded to Jersey but it has not stopped French adventurers from invading in 1984 and 1998. One colourful episode was when Jean Raspail, a French royalist and writer, claimed the island on behalf of the government of his Majesty Orelie-Antoine I, King of Araucania and Patagonia... the only problem being that the King (in fact a French explorer called Antoine de Tounens who had proclaimed himself a king) had been dead for 130 years.

Elizabeth Castle, St Helier

Albert Harbour, St Helier

Havre des Pas Bathing Pool

Quetivel Mill, National
Trust for Jersey

LEFT Tesson Mill, National Trust for Jersey
BELOW Noirmont Point

RIGHT AND BELOW Noirmont Point

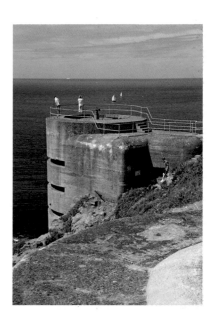

LEFT St Brelade Parish Hall in the old
railway station building at St Aubin
BELOW St Aubin Harbour

RIGHT Ouaisne Bay
BELOW Martello tower, Ouaisne Bay

St Brelade Bay

Church of St Brelade and
Fisherman's Chapel

Jersey lavender, St Brelade

La Corbière Lighthouse

Rocks at Corbière Point

La Rocco Tower at St Ouen's Bay

La Caumine à Marie Best, an old guard house on the western side of Le Chemin de L'Ouzière, St Ouen.

St Ouen's Pond

St Ouen's Bay

Sand-yachting at St Ouen's Bay

Les Landes overlooking
St Ouen's Bay

View towards St Ouen's Bay

Grosnez Castle

Cliffs seen from Grosnez Castle

Plemont Bay

Grève De Lecq Bay

Bonne Nuit Bay

Bonne Nuit Bay

Fort Crete

Bouley Bay

Fliquet Bay

St Catherine's Breakwater

Archirondel Tower

La Pouquelaye de Faldouet
Dolmen, Faldouet

RIGHT La Hougue Bie
(courtesy of La Société Jersiaise and Jersey Heritage)
BELOW Mont Orgueil Castle, Gorey

La Rocque Harbour

Le Hocq Tower

Low tide near Le Hocq Tower

Green Island, off Jersey

Castle Cornet, St Peter Port

Guernsey

GUERNSEY

The island of Guernsey is the second largest of the Channel Islands. As in Jersey, Neolithic man settled here and created many defensive earthworks, dolmens and menhirs. The oldest burial mound is Les Fouillages, which is possibly the oldest man-made structure in Europe. Guernsey's main town is the cosmopolitan St Peter Port, which started out as a small fishing village. This neat and well-planned town with predominantly Georgian and Regency townhouses, multi-level gardens and chic streets, owed its prosperity in the seventeenth and eighteenth centuries to privateering, maritime trade in the nineteenth, and in the twentieth-century, the development of financial services. The historic royal fortress, Castle Cornet, guards the entrance to St Peter Port. Today the fortress houses three museums, as well as perfect examples of gardens from various periods. The castle's history spans eight centuries. It was built in the twelfth century by the English Crown, after King John lost Normandy. Castle Cornet was built on the islet, and it was only in the late eighteenth century, that the Castle Pier linking the fortress to St Peter Port, as well as the lighthouse, was added. Its present form is the result of Tudor renovations in the sixteenth century, following the plans of John Rogers and later by Paul Ivy. There are many performances and events held in the castle and the Napoleonic gun is fired daily.

It is only a short walk from the castle to the centre of town with its old quarters meticulously preserved cobbled streets, elegant art galleries and antiques shops. Nearby are the Victorian Candie Gardens where the oldest heated glass-houses in the British Isles can be found. Other places worth visiting are the twelfth-century parish church of St Peter Port and Hauteville House, home of the great writer and even greater eccentric, Victor Hugo. Hugo spent fourteen years in exile from France here, and it was here that he wrote the novel *Les Miserables*.

Apart from St Peter Port the island has many fascinating places to visit. The island's stately home of Sausmarez has been the home of Seigneurs de Sausmarez for eight hundred years. Full of interesting paintings and tapestries, the house is well worth a visit, if not for its beauty then for its fascinating ghost stories as it is possibly the most haunted house in Britain. The house is surrounded by subtropical gardens and decorated with an impressive collection of contemporary sculpture. Saumarez Park is a lovely park open for visitors. Plenty of attractive trees shade the elegant house that is currently a retirement home. At Les Vauxbelets is the little chapel built in 1923 by Brother Déodat entirely from broken pottery and shells; it is a miniature version of the famous grotto and basilica at Lourdes in France.

Fort Grey on the west coast of the island is a Napoleonic martello tower built in 1804. Locally known as 'the cup and saucer', it currently houses the Shipwreck Museum. Many fascinating maritime relics and artefacts from ships and boats wrecked in Channel Island waters are displayed here. Some of the most dangerous rocks on the west coast of Guernsey are near Les Hanois. Victor Hugo described them as: "These rocks – these midnight assassins have filled the cemeteries of Tortavel and Rocquaine". Fort Grey stands on the rock and the site of a previous castle, Chateau de Rocquaine. Fort Grey was supposedly the favourite meeting place of local witches. The dolmens and ancient graves scattered all over the island are relics from Neolithic times. The tallest menhir of three and a half metres (11.5ft) is La Longue Rocque. According to local folklore, it was a fairy's favourite cricket bat; other legends claim that touching it increases fertility. La Verde on Mont Cuet Road is a ten-metre-long (33-foot) passage grave from 3,000 BC. Even older is Les Fouillages Neolithic burial chamber on L'Ancresse. Pleinmont is the place where the 'Fairy Ring', a fascinating round table dug in the ground, is positioned. Local legend suggests that your wish will come true if you walk three times around. The 'Fairy Ring' most probably dates from the seventeenth century when it was used by the 'Pions', companions to the officials of the Royal Court during a Chevauchee parade, held every two years to ensure the *Chemin du Roi* or path of the King was kept clear.

German occupation left the island heavily fortified. Defensive positions, a part of Hitler's grand plan of the Atlantic Wall, are visible all around the coast. Some, like Pleinmont Tower, a five-storey observation tower in Torteval at Pleinmont or Fort Hommet in Vazon Bay are open to visitors. Another reminder of the Occupation is the German Military Underground Hospital, the largest construction in the Channel Islands dug into solid rock by slave labour. These vast subterranean concrete tunnels hide grim remains – the dead bodies of the prisoners of war who died here while working in inhuman conditions are buried in the cement walls of the tunnels.

Guernsey offers some most spectacular coastal walks and a selection of fabulous beaches. There are some five hundred kilometres (310 miles) of roads and lanes for walking; cliff paths with an ever-changing coastline, the fabulous beaches of Cobo and Vazon, as well as picturesque coves and rocks, like the famous Moulin Houet painted by French impressionist Pierre Auguste Renoir in 1883.

Off the west coast of Guernsey, at L'Eree headland is Lihou, a twenty-hectare tidal island. This tranquil place, abundant in marine life, had a long association with the Benedictine monks of Mont St Michael. The Priory of St Mary was established here in 1114. Over the centuries, the island passed through various tenants before ending up in the hands of the State of Guernsey who purchased it as an open nature reserve. The island can be explored at low tide by a quarter-mile ancient stone causeway. Many sea birds nest on the island: oyster-catchers, ringed plovers, gulls, gannets, egrets plus others. The Priory fell into decay in the sixteenth century and is currently a ruin. Lihou was used by the locals in the past for seaweed harvesting and in 1927 a small factory producing iodine was even established here. The original farmhouse on the island had to be replaced after the war, as it was used as a target for German artillery. This tranquil island is currently run by the Lihou Charitable Trust and it is an important site of nature conservation that is open to the public, with the exception of some restricted bird nesting areas.

Left battery at Vazon Bay

Constitution Steps, St Peter Port

Victorian pillar box, the oldest posting box in
the British Isles, Union Street, St Peter Port

Victoria Tower, St Peter Port, dating from 1848, marks the Queen's first visit to Guernsey.

Queen Victoria statue and Priaulx Library in Candie Gardens, St Peter Port

Castle Cornet, St Peter Port

Castle Pier and a lighthouse, St Peter Port

St Peter Port

Victoria Marina, St Peter Port

Sausmarez Manor House

Little Chapel

Petit Bot Bay

Petit Bot Waterfall

The Underground Hospital

Pleinmont Observation Tower

Pleinmont Battery

Les Hanois Lighthouse and Les
Hanois rocks

LEFT Fort Pezeries
BELOW La Table des Pions – 'Fairy Ring'

Fort Grey with 18th-century anchor

L'Eree Bay

Lihou Island off Guernsey

Fort Saumarez

LEFT Le Trépied dolmen
BELOW Mont Chinchon Battery

St Apolline Chapel

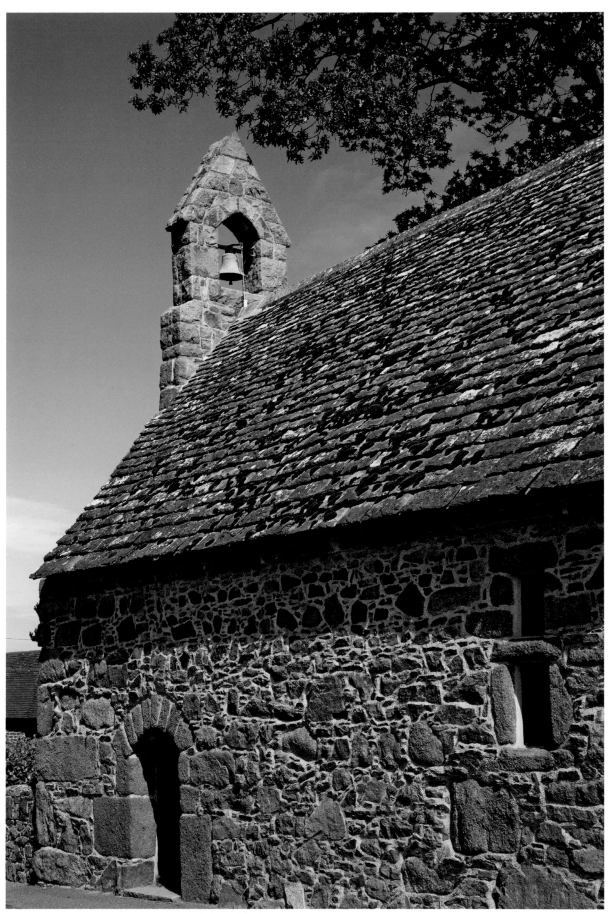

Vazon Bay

Vazon Bay

Vazon Bay

Saumarez Park

Grandes Rocques

Grandes Rocques

Cobo Bay

Le Grand Havre

Creux Harbour, Sark

Sark and Herm

SARK

Sark is the smallest of the four main Channel Islands. This picturesque island is located 129 kilometres (80 miles) south of the English coast and is accessible by boat from Guernsey. The natural beauty of its spectacular coastline, the sheer cliff drops and abundance of flowers and seabird colonies make this island a fascinating place to visit. The island is 5 kilometres (3 miles) long and 2.4 kilometres (a mile and a half) wide. Originally inhabited by the Veneti tribe, the island was annexed by the Roman Empire around 56 BC. In 933 it became a part of the Duchy of Normandy. In later years it was used by monastic communities as well as pirates. It was only in 1565 that Queen Elizabeth I granted the island of Sark to Helier de Carteret as a *fief haubert*. Since that time it was directly responsible to the Crown, a unique state that it retained until the twenty-first century. Helier de Carteret became the first Seigneur and his role was to protect the island along with forty men equipped with musket; theoretically the tenants of today are still required to keep a musket to defend Sark! The island is the smallest independent state in the Commonwealth and until 2008 was ruled by its Seigneur under a constitution dating back to Elizabethan times and it was the only feudal state in Europe. Sark converted overnight from sixteenth-century feudal law into a democracy after Sir Frederick Barclay and his brother, Sir David, took the island to the European Court of Human Rights. The ruling against the law of promogeniture of Sark changed centuries of tradition. Although new laws were introduced some of the old laws are still valid; the most famous one is the old Norman custom of *Clameur de Haro*. This ancient custom of 'crying for justice', mainly when property is being threatened, works as a kind of an injunction. It requires the *criant* to go down on one knee in front of witnesses and raise a *clameur* by reciting the Lord's Prayer in French and crying out: *"Haro, Haro, Haro! A' mon aide mon Prince, on me fait tort!"* (Haro, Haro, Haro!, to my aid my Prince, I am being wronged). The raising of the *clameur* acts as a temporary injunction and the issue is dealt with by the court. Another unique law is that only the Seigneur of Sark can keep doves and an unspayed dog. Some inquisitive visitors also try to establish if the *Droit de Seigneur* law (a privilege of sleeping with a bride on the wedding night) is valid here, but so far there is no evidence of it!

Originally a fishing and farming community, Sark was transformed into a tourist paradise in the Victorian era. A mild climate, 64.5 kilometres (40 miles) of picturesque coastlines, splendid cliffs, caves and many convenient hotels make it the perfect holiday base. A small population of around 600 inhabitants is scattered over the island. Cars are not allowed but tractors are used for agriculture and transport. Visitors enjoy using bicycles and horse-drawn carriages even more. The 'Avenue', the main street at the top of the Harbour Hill and its selection of shops and cafés looks like a film set. Most people in the island speak English, but official documents are written in French and the older generation can still speak Serquiaise. The police and fire service operate on an unpaid voluntary basis. The last time the local policeman had to intervene was in 1991, when an eccentric French nuclear physicist equipped with a semi–automatic weapon attempted an invasion. There is a tiny prison on this laid back island but minor offenders can escape detention on condition they wear a t-shirt emblazoned with the word 'Prisoner' on the back.

La Seigneurie is the official home of the Seigneur of Sark. Built on the site of the sixth-century St Magloire Monastery, the house has been altered over the years. It has an impressive Victorian tower and beautifully tended garden with exotic and local plants, which is open to the public. The top visitors' attraction is La Coupée (The Knife), the spectacular isthmus joining Great Sark to Little Sark. This natural causeway is 90 metres long (295 ft) and has a drop of a hundred metres (328 ft) on both sides. An amazing view of Grande Grêve beach is visible from the top. The concrete road and protective railings were built in 1945. Little Sark is also worth a visit as it houses the remains of copper and silver mines as well as two spectacular natural pools, the Venus pool and the Adonis pool.

Brecqhou, the rocky 64 hectare- (160-acre) islet is difficult to distinguish when first approaching by sea as it blends into the neighbouring island of Sark. The most famous characteristic of the island is the spectacular honey-coloured Fort Brecqhou. Visible for miles, this gothic-style castle with towers, spires, fortified walls and a moat is not a relic of the past, but an extensive cliff-top residence built by the famous Barclay twin brothers after they bought the island in 1993. The multi-millionaire media magnates created a stir in the neighbouring island of Sark, not due to the construction of this castle but by objecting to the centuries-old laws and traditions governing both islands. Legal disputes with the government of Sark started with the demand of the repayment of the *trezime* property tax, and were followed by a challenge to the law of primogeniture (where the first born male has the right of inheritance). However, the most significant legal challenge was for the abolition of the feudal system of Sark in order to introduce democracy. Mr Beaumount, until recently the Seigneur of Sark, was formally the feudal Lord and the island was the last bastion of feudalism in the western world. In 2008 the feudal system was abolished and a democratic government was elected. The island's subjects had never opposed medieval rule, as their archaic system was not oppressive and worked well; eventually they grudgingly accepted the new laws. The Barclay brothers guard their privacy ferociously so unfortunately neither the castle nor the immaculate park can be viewed by the public.

There are many small islands of Sark: Bec du Nez, L'Etac, Noire Pierre, Petit Moie, Grande Moie, Moie de Port Gorey, Moie de la Bretagne.

Lighthouse at Point Robert

View from La Maseline Harbour

Coastline near Point Robert

Local transport

The Seigneurie Gardens

Grande Grêve Beach

La Coupée

Fishing equipment

Creux Harbour

Brecqhou Island off Sark

HERM

Herm is a small island, approximately 2.4 kilometres (1.5 miles) long and less than a kilometre (half a mile) wide, positioned 4.8 kilometres (3 miles) from Guernsey. This tiny island has been occupied from prehistoric times. The island was considered a sacred place and many Neolithic tombs have been found scattered around. Unfortunately a lot of the tombs were damaged or completely destroyed in the nineteenth century when the island was quarried for granite. In the sixth century Catholic monks established a monastic sanctuary here. Most probably, the name 'Herm' derives from the hermits who settled here. The tiny tenth-century St Tugual Church on the hill above Spring Meadow, was built to commemorate the death of a Welsh woman who died here during her trip to Guernsey with St Magloire. Stained windows in the chapel are a relatively new addition as they were commissioned by Major Peter Wood who looked after the island between 1949 and 1980. In medieval times the island served as a hunting ground for the governors of Guernsey. Nineteenth-century industry brought its granite quarries as well as copper and silver mines. Granite taken from the island was used in many prominent buildings in London, including the steps of St Paul's Cathedral, which are made from granite quarried on the Le Monceau Hill. Before the First World War, an eccentric Prussian prince, Blücher von Wahlstaff, grandson of the famous Prussian field marshall who helped the Duke of Wellington defeat Napoleon at Waterloo, bought the island lease and transformed it into his personal kingdom. He introduced a colony of wallabies here; none now survive, but the manor house still has a teutonic look due to the the extensions and castellated decor he added. The next well-known tenant on the island was writer, Compton Mackenzie, who wrote *Monarch of the Glen* and *Whisky Galore*. The island spent much of the Second World War under German occupation, but it was relatively undisturbed by the occupiers; no fortifications were built and only the beaches were used for landing practices. After the war, the State of Guernsey bought Herm from the Crown and now rents the island to tenants.

Today, Herm is a holiday destination famous for its crystal clear, turquoise waters, sandy beaches, hidden bays and large dunes. This idyllic island is free of crowds and cars as well. A cluster of cottages, small shops, some restaurants, two campsites and one hotel cater for all the tourists' needs. Mild springs and long summers allow subtropical plants and wild flowers to flourish on the island. Herm is swarming with birds; 92 species were identified here by the Ornithological Society including puffins, razorbills, shags, oyster-catchers, terns and guillemots. A favourite beach on the island is Shell Beach, where millions of shells have been deposited by the Gulf Stream. The island would not be complete without its own ghost: according to Major Wood, who is mainly responsible for the way the island is today, a sixteenth-century monk walks the island. All of this contributes to Herm's unofficial title of 'The Jewel in the Channel Islands' Crown'.

Positioned south of Herm is the small island of Jethou. A severe storm in AD 709 washed away a narrow strip of land connecting the island with the neighbouring larger island of Herm. The old viking name of this place, *Keitholm* meaning 'The Roaring Place' most probably originated from the noise of the air forced through the *Creux du Diable* passage (Devil's Hole passage). For such a small island it has a very colourful history. Dolmens and menhir indicate that the island was inhabited very early on. Bequeathed to the monastery of Mont St Michael, it was taken away from the monks by Henry V only to be left uninhabited for many years and consequently Herm became a favourite haunt of pirates. In the fight against the pirates, the authorities started to hang criminals on the summit of Jethou as a deterrent. Quarried for granite, used as storage for brandy smuggling, the island changed hands often. In 1948 a café was opened here, but as drinks were typically served outside licensing hours, it was famously raided by Guernsey police in 1954 and closed. Jethou Island is home to much wildlife, particularly of the bird variety. Apart from the colourful puffins nesting in the eastern cliff top, it is also used by gulls, cormorants, shags, oyster-catchers, guillemots and many others. Plenty of rabbits inhabit the island but it is lacking mice, squirrels, hedgehogs and other mammals. The island offers spectacular views, colourful rocks on the east coast, secluded bays, beaches and impressive boulders as well as 'Fairy Wood', which in the spring becomes spectacularly carpeted with a mass of flowering bluebells.

Other small islets in the vicinity of Herm are: Crevichon, Les Houmets, Grande Amfroque, Grande Fauconniere, Hermetier, Coquarobert, Putrainez and Selle Roque.

Herm Harbour

Herm village

The Ship Inn

Bear's Beach

CLOCKWISE FROM TOP LEFT:
Neolithic graves near Bear's Beach;
Marram grass; Sea-holly;
Pierre aux Rats Obelisk

St Tugual Church

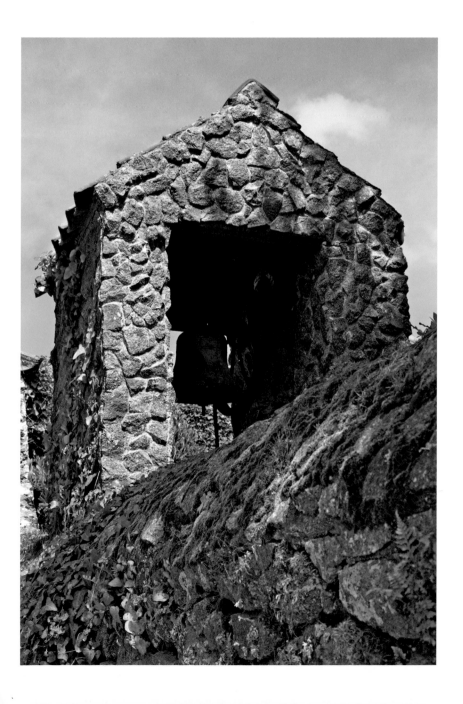

Manor House

Alderney Point

Shell Beach

Breakwater, Braye Bay

Alderney

ALDERNEY

Alderney is the third largest and the most northerly of the Channel Islands. It is 4.8 kilometres (three miles) long and 2.4 kilometres (one and a half miles) wide and it is only 11 kilometres (7 miles) off the coast of Normandy. The island has been inhabited since Neolithic times, although much of the traces from this era, such as dolmens, were lost during periods of extensive fortifications of the island. Some of the most significant Neolithic sites are near Fort Tourgis and on Longis Common. The island is notorious for its fierce current, the Swinge, between Alderney and Burhou, and Le Raz, between the island and the Normandy mainland. These currents, together with severe tides and dangerous coastline, have claimed many ships and boats. Alderney has developed slowly over the centuries and even today it remains unspoiled and peaceful. The importance of Alderney grew rapidly in the nineteenth century when a huge breakwater and thirteen forts were built in an attempt to counteract constant attacks from Normandy and Brittany. The massive breakwater in Braye harbour was designed by James Walker and constructed between 1847–64. Originally 1,430 metres (over 4,500 feet) long, it was big enough to shelter the entire Channel Islands' fleet. The breakwater was originally 16 metres (52 feet) high and about 12 metres (39 feet) wide, but it has suffered regular damage during storms and so today it is only 870 metres (over 2,800 feet) long. The stone for the building of the breakwater was carried to Braye harbour by a special railway. One of the peculiarities of this railway was that all locomotives were equipped with life belts. The requirement was imposed after one of the engines failed to stop at the end of the breakwater and continued into the sea. This is the only railway in all of the Channel Islands and today it is run by volunteers and open to summer visitors for rides. The diesel engine pulls two London Underground carriages from the harbour to Mannez Quarry.

Alderney was under German occupation between 1940–45. The entire population left the island and German troops established four concentration camps here for slave labour. Prisoners were used to build bunkers, towers, shelters and all kinds of fortifications that formed part of Hitler's Atlantic Wall. Today, the Hammonds Memorial commemorates all the workers who died and were buried above Longis Common.

The main, and only town, in Alderney is St Anne, with a population of 2,400 residents. St Anne, or simply called 'Town' or 'La Ville', is located in the centre of the island. It is a vibrant place, especially in the summer, when tourists visit this charming historic town with its cobbled streets and Georgian colour-washed houses. The main tourist attraction and must-see for all visitors is the church of St Anne designed by George Gilbert Scott. Scott was the Victorian architect most famous for the Midland Grand Hotel in St Pancras, London and the Albert Memorial in Hyde Park, London. The church was completed in 1850 and due to its size is often called 'the Cathedral of the Channel Islands'. Also worth visiting is the local museum, where relics of a wreck, possibly the Elizabethan warship *Makeshift* are displayed. This is the only Elizabethan warship ever found, and it sank off Alderney in 1592. The *Makeshift* was a Pinnace from Drake's squadron, part of the fleet that defended England from the Armada and it was 18.2 metres (60 feet) in length and 70 tons in weight.

Another interesting place to visit is the Alderney (or Mannez) Lighthouse at Quesnard Point. Offering spectacular views and visible from far away, this thirty-two metre (104ft) structure built in 1912 was essential for navigation. It helped many ships avoid disaster in the treacherous tidal ranges and strong currents. The charm of the island lies not only in its landscape and the architecture of St Anne, but also in its wildlife. Although Alderney lacks trees, as they were first cut down in the seventeenth century to fuel the lighthouses and then during the Nazi occupation, it has an abundance of flora and fauna with almost three hundred species of birds. The most famous Alderney mammal is an extremely rare and distinctive blonde hedgehog. There are over one thousand pairs of these hedgehogs, which are not albinos but a genetic variant. They have black eyes, are very cute and placid and they do not carry fleas. Other unusual residents on Alderney are black rabbits. They are the largest mammals inhabiting the island and a lack of natural predators ensures their survival.

Just over 3 kilometres (2 miles) to the north of Alderney is Burhou Island, a listed bird sanctuary. This low-lying island has a colony of puffins. The rabbit holes make good nesting for these lovely birds. Other birds nesting on the island are oyster-catchers, shags, storm petrels and gulls. Visiting the island is prohibited during the puffin nesting season (from the end of March until 26th July), as the numbers of puffins has declined dramatically in the last two decades. On the rocks near Burhou there are colonies of Northern Gannets and some grey seals can be spotted resting there. An interesting eight-metre (26-ft) raised beach in the north-east part of the island is a relic of the Ice Age. Burhou has no human inhabitants and no natural source of drinking water but there has been a hut here since 1820. Built as a shelter for fishermen and shipwrecked mariners, it was destroyed by German artillery who used it for target practice. The hut was replaced in 1953 and can be rented out for a small fee. The area around the island is littered with shipwrecks.

A series of dangerous, strangely-shaped rocks called the Casquets are positioned west of Alderney. Until the seventeenth century they were called Les Gattes Hazes and later the name was changed to the Casquets. Many lives have been lost on and around the dreaded rocks, hence the name 'Graveyard of the English Channel'. One of the earliest recorded losses was Prince William of Normandy, the son and heir of Henry I, who was travelling on the *White Ship* when it sank in 1120. So dangerous were the rocks that, after the loss of the frigate *Album*, it was decided that a lighthouse was needed there. In 1723 Thomas Le Cocq, the owner of the rocks, ordered the construction of three towers with coal lights. The towers, however, were only 9 metres (30 ft) high, and therefore not visible enough in heavy storms. This was probably the reason behind the greatest calamity, the sinking in 1744 of HMS *Victory*, Lord Nelson's predecessor. HMS *Victory*, the 'finest ship in the world' as it was known then, sank with 900 sailors, 200 mariners and 50 volunteers, including members of the most powerful families in England. *Victory*, the most technically advanced vessel of the time was on her way back from a rescue mission of the Mediteranean convoy. To lose the most respected admiral, Sir John Balchin and so many experienced sailors, was a dramatic loss for the British Navy, compounded by the financial loss of something in the region of one billion pounds in today's money. In February 2009, the ship was found by the Odyssey Marine Exploration Company and the long-lasting mystery of the ship's demise and its location will soon be revealed.

Another heavy loss in these waters happened in 1899, when the steamer SS *Stella* struck the Casquets and the bottom of the hull was torn open. She sank within eight minutes along with over one hundred people. The fog on this fatal day was so heavy that the keeper of the lighthouse was unaware of the tragedy unfolding nearby. The heroism of the people involved and the dramatic loss of so many sparked great interest in the press. The towers of the lighthouse were raised twice and only the North West Tower is currently in use. The East Tower contains the foghorn and the South West Tower is used as a helipad.

There are also other isles off Alderney: Romonquet, Ortac, Les Etacs, Nannels, Coque Lihou and many smaller rocks.

Carved puffin

Harbour, Braye Bay

Jetty, Braye Beach

CLOCKWISE FROM TOP LEFT:
Entrance to Alderney Museum, St Anne;
Tower of the Old Church and the site of the island's first
school, St Anne; St Anne Church; Rue de Braye

Island Hall

Fort Houmet Herbe

Ruins of Fort Les Homeaux Florains

Saye Bay

Blue Bay

Mannez Quarry bird hide

Mannez Lighthouse at Quesnard Point

Longis Bay and Ile de Raz Fort

Les Etacs seen from Giffoine

Cliff path near Vallée des Trois Vaux

Gannet colony on Les Etacs

Fort Clonque

RIGHT Roc à l'Épine, a Neolithic burial chamber overlooking Platte Saline Bay
BELOW Fort Tourgis

Burhou Island bird sanctuary, off Alderney

Puffins on Burhou Island, off Alderney

Sunset over Great Nannel, off Alderney

INDEX